First U.S. Edition 1982 by Barron's Educational Series, Inc.

First published in 1977 by
Skolförlaget AB Gävle Sweden
© Grethe Fagerström and Gunilla Hansson
and Skolförlaget AB 1977

First published in the English Language edition by
Macdonald Educational Limited
Test this edition © Macdonald Educational Limited 1979

All inquiries should be addressed to:
Barron's Educational Series, Inc.
113 Crossways Park Drive
Woodbury, New York 11797
Library of Congress Catalog Card No. 82-3892
International Book No. 0-8120-5458-X

Library of Congress Cataloging in Publication Data

Fagerström, Grethe, 1916-
  Our new baby.
  Originally published: Gävle, Skolförlaget AB, 1977.
  Summary: Peter and Lucy's parents explain reproduction
and childbirth in order to prepare them for the arrival
of a new baby.
  1. Sex instruction for children. 2. Children's
questions and answers. [1. Sex instruction for children.
2. Childbirth. 3. Babies] I. Hansson, Gunilla, ill.
II. Title.
HQ53.F33 1982   649'.65   82-3892
ISBN 0-8120-5458-X   AACR2

PRINTED IN HONG KONG

23456   041   987654321

Our New Baby

a picture story for parents and children

written by Grethe Fagerström
and Gunilla Hansson

illustrated by Gunilla Hansson

Barron's
Woodbury, New York

Foreword

This book tells in an easy conversational tone the story of Peter and Lucy Williams, who are going to have a new brother or sister.

It is not always easy for adults to answer children's questions about sex either truthfully or directly. Prejudices and prohibitions from childhood often stand in the way and generate uneasiness.

Respected expert opinion says that in spite of sex instruction being available to many children, most of them are going to form their own ideas and interpretations of what adults have said or read to them. This is because children have neither the experience nor the physical maturity to understand the complexities of sexual interplay. We should not worry if we notice that a child has not properly understood what has been said or has even distorted it, since more opportunities will arise later to inform the child in the right context. The children in this story ask questions and give their own opinions at their own pace, when it seems appropriate to them.

Today's children live in varying types of family structures, and in Peter and Lucy's block of apartments there are several different kinds of families. Living together in a family is hard work. Every family has bad days when tiredness and ill temper take over and nothing goes right. This is also true of the Williams family. By describing different types of emotions, such as anger, happiness, jealousy, solidarity, we hope that both adults and children will feel that every sort of emotion is part of daily life and needs to be expressed. We have even briefly taken up the consumer society's pressure on families with children.

Peter and Lucy's questions and their parents' answers provide the context for other questions or discussion at the end of each chapter. The children work through their new experiences, often in the form of play, make comparisons, and find their own solutions. We hope that these discussion pages create new questions which in their turn will lead to practical and truthful conversations between child and adult. We want children to feel that they are taken seriously, that adults listen to them, answer their questions, and respect their games. But above all we want this book to help children and adults feel that sexuality is a natural and positive part of their lives.

By using a cartoon format, we have given children who have not yet learned to read the opportunity of looking back at different pictures on their own and re-experiencing the story through them. BUT IT IS IMPORTANT THAT THE BOOK FIRST BE READ TOGETHER WITH AN ADULT IN WHOM THE CHILD HAS COMPLETE CONFIDENCE.

Grethe Fagerström
Gunilla Hansson

Contents

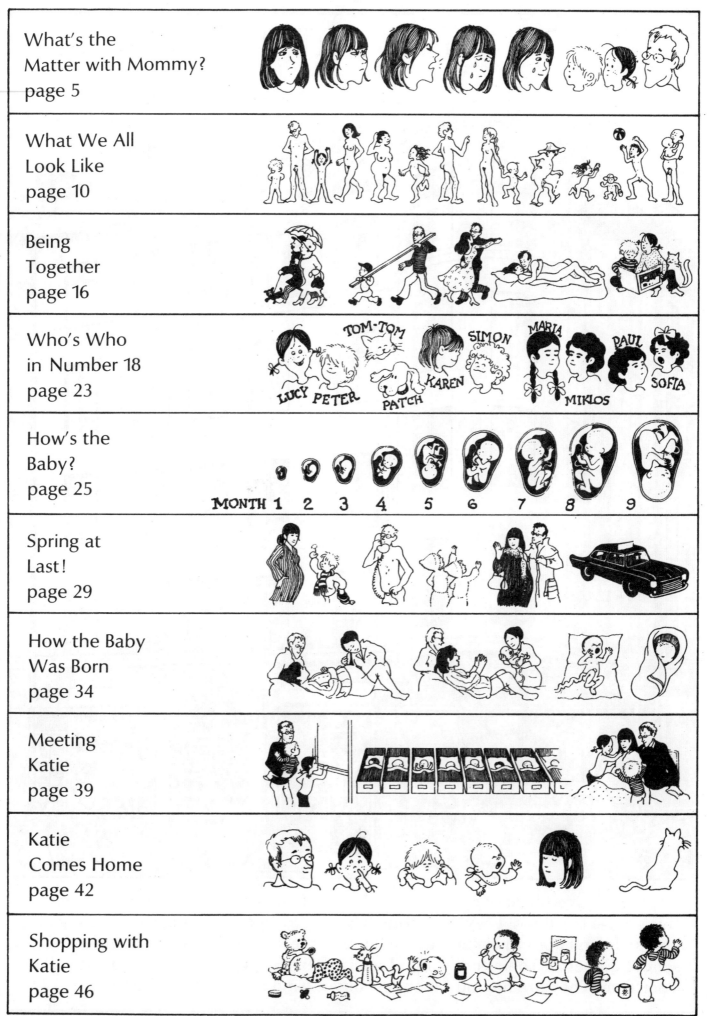

Number 18 is a block of apartments. Robert, Lisa, Lucy, and Peter Williams live on the top floor. They have four rooms, a kitchen and a bath. Lucy is eight years old and goes to elementary school. Peter is five and goes to nursery school. Robert is their daddy, and Lisa is their mommy. They have a cat called Tom-Tom. They are having lunch one day during summer vacation.

There are lots of things up in the attic. There is a big box with LUCY and PETER written on the side.

It can't be so expensive. There are lots of clothes here. I wore this. The baby can have it. I wonder what we'll call it?

Look, Lucy! What scruffy little shoes. The baby won't want these.

Do you think it is expensive having a new baby?
Does it cost more having older children?
Why do you think the family saved those old shoes?
Have you anything saved from when you were little?

What We All Look Like

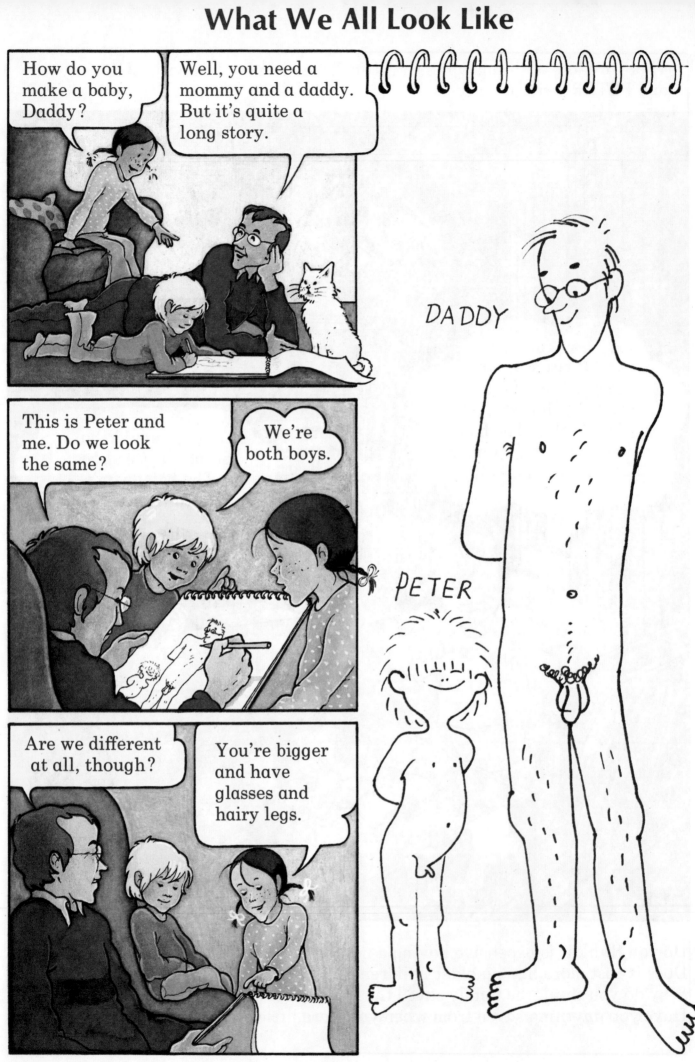

Lucy draws herself, and Daddy draws Mommy.

Do you think we look the same at all?

We've both got brown eyes and long hair.

Are we different in any way, then?

You've got big bosoms and a bit of hairy tummy.

Lucy's and my bosoms are the same size.

Mine will be bigger than yours when I grow up.

MOMMY

LUCY

Yes, that's right. There must be room for milk in case you have a baby one day.

Lucy and I have two little holes between our legs. Under the little hole where we urinate is another little hole that is the entrance to the vagina. The vagina leads to a special place that all girls have in their tummies. It's called the womb. The womb is where our new baby is at the moment.

A baby lies in its mommy's womb before it is born. When the baby is ready to come out, it slides down the vagina and out of the little hole.

On each side of the womb is a place where egg cells are kept. Egg cells are needed for a woman to have babies.

This is what an egg cell looks like under a microscope.

13

14

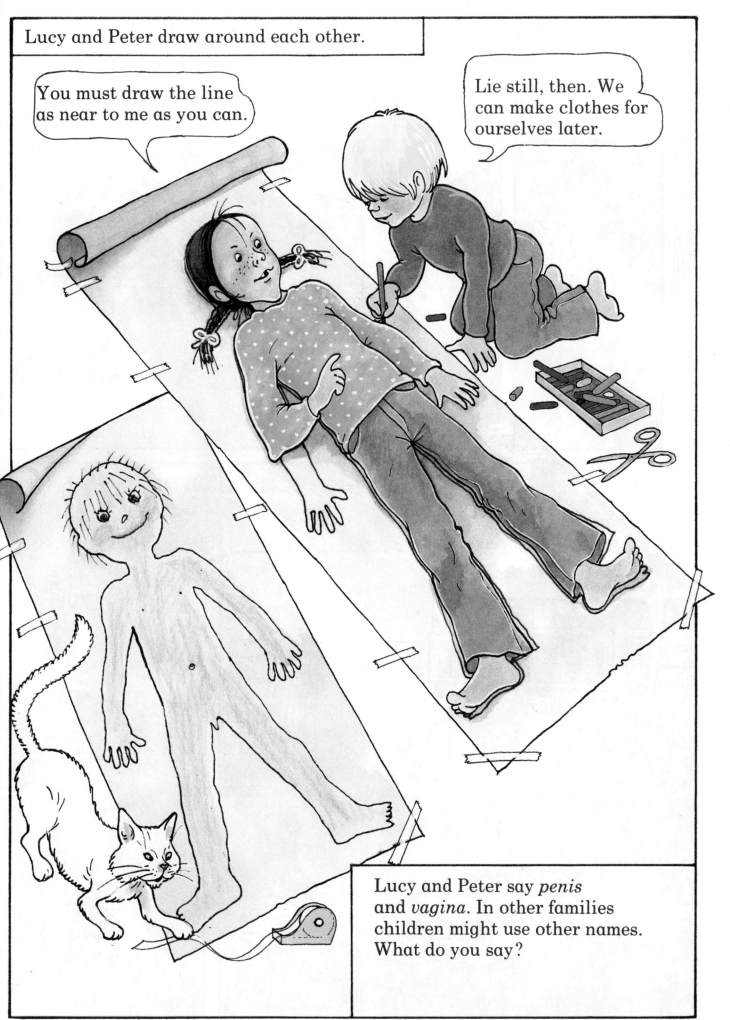

Lucy and Peter draw around each other.

You must draw the line as near to me as you can.

Lie still, then. We can make clothes for ourselves later.

Lucy and Peter say *penis* and *vagina*. In other families children might use other names. What do you say?

Being Together

Because making love with Mommy felt really terrific, I ejaculated, which means I let lots of sperm cells into Mommy's vagina.

They swam up into the womb and met an egg cell on its way down.

Here are the sperm cells swimming really fast. There are both boy and girl sperms. Here comes the egg cell! They are going to meet soon.

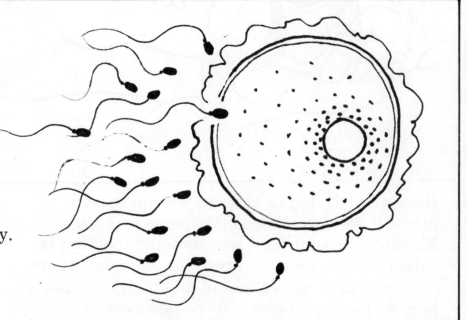

The egg cell lets in only one sperm, and we don't know if it was a boy or a girl. We shall have to wait until the baby arrives. The sperm cell burrowed its way into the egg cell and made one new cell. This cell was the beginning of the new baby.

20

How many times have you and Daddy made love?

Lots of times.

But we don't make a baby every time. If we did, we would have far too many children to look after.

A baby can start to grow only if the egg and the sperm join up with each other and the new cell stays in the womb and begins to grow. But we can keep the sperm and egg from meeting if we want to by using various things called contraceptives.

So you see, Daddy and I can make love lots of times without making a baby if we want to.

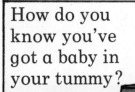

How do you know you've got a baby in your tummy?

No, not yet. But my periods have stopped. They disappear when a woman is expecting a baby.

The doctor examined me and said there was a baby there.

Can you feel it?

Why weren't we at the party?

I was very happy, and in the evening Daddy and I had a party.

What did you say then?

It was very late, and you were in bed fast asleep.

Who's Who in Number 18

Soon everyone will be asleep.

good morning!

It's Sunday morning, and everyone in Number 18 is waking up.

Mike and Maggie Clark live next to Peter and Lucy. They are still asleep, but their little dog Patch is awake.

Simon is nine years old. He lives on the third floor with his daddy. Simon has made coffee.

Karen lives on the second floor with her mommy. Today is her birthday. She is six years old and is going to have a party.

And this is the Heritakis family. Maria and Miklos are twins. They are in the same class as Lucy. Kosta is Peter's friend. They live on the first floor with baby Sofia, Mom, Dad, and Gran.

The children are playing in the playground behind the apartment building.
Where do you play? Where do your friends live?
Who do some of your friends live with—mother, father, both parents, others?

How's the Baby?

Daddy draws a picture and explains.

This is the baby at six months old moving about in Mommy's womb. The womb has gotten bigger so that the baby has plenty of room.

This is the placenta. That's the baby's pantry. When Mommy eats, some of the goodness goes there for the baby.

This is the umbilical cord. The baby gets air and food through that. When the baby is born, its belly button will show where the cord was attached.

How does it go to the bathroom?

It just urinates sometimes, that's all!

What's it like having such a big tummy?

Spring at Last!

Lucy has made a list of all the things baby Katie will need.

Do you think I have forgotten anything?

NO! Tom-Tom, you must keep out of Katie's bed.

What does a new baby need?
Has Lucy forgotten anything?
What would you call a new brother or sister?
Do you ever have baby-sitters?

How the Baby Was Born

We went to the hospital in a taxi. There is a ward where all the babies are.

Mommy put on a big shirt and warm socks. Then the doctor came and listened to the baby's heart. She said it was fine.

Katie was pushing all the time to come out. The waterproof bag had broken now, and the water came out. There wasn't much time left to wait.

It's hard work having a baby, and towards the end it hurt. Mommy and I held each other's hands tightly. Even though it hurt, it was very exciting waiting for a new baby. We waited in a room like a bedroom, though in some hospitals Mommy would have gone to the kind of room where operations are performed.

Then the doctor said she could see the baby's head. I had a quick look. I could just see the top of Katie's head. Mommy gave one last big push. The doctor helped, and—the baby started to appear.

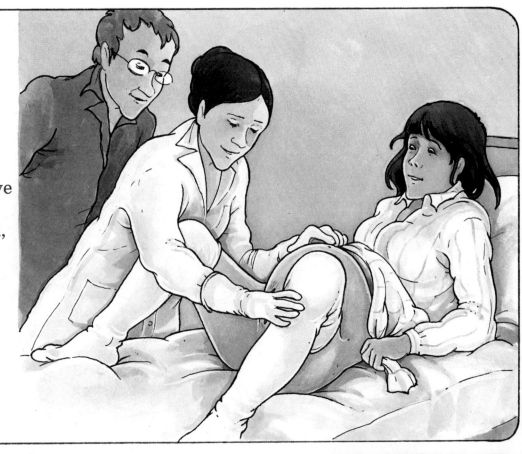

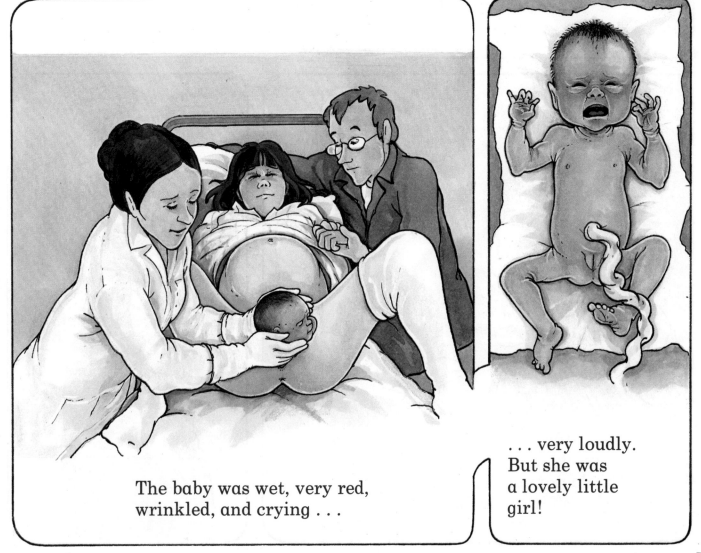

The baby was wet, very red, wrinkled, and crying . . .

. . . very loudly. But she was a lovely little girl!

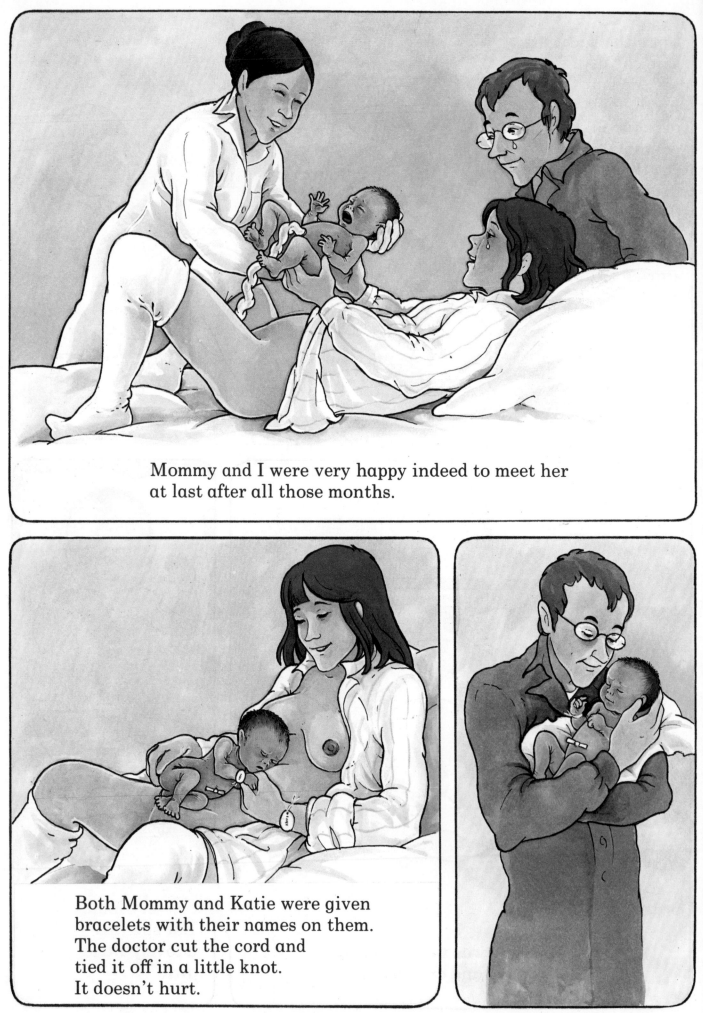

Mommy and I were very happy indeed to meet her
at last after all those months.

Both Mommy and Katie were given
bracelets with their names on them.
The doctor cut the cord and
tied it off in a little knot.
It doesn't hurt.

A male nurse gave Katie a bath.

Then she was weighed and . . .

. . . measured. Everything about her was written on a card.

The doctor examined her, and then she was dressed in some tiny clothes . . .

a little shirt

a diaper

pants

and a warm blanket

Then she was ready for a nap.

Mommy got some clean clothes, and then we had a cup of tea.

Mommy held Katie and I carefully lay on the bed and we watched her sleeping. Then I came home to you two.

How could Katie get out of that little hole?

The hole can stretch just like a rubber band. Then it gets little again.

That afternoon Peter, Daddy, and Lucy look at old family photographs.
Do you ever look at old family photographs?

Have you a photograph of yourself as a baby?
Have you a photograph of your mother or father as a baby?
What sort of clothes did they wear?

Meeting Katie

Have you ever seen a newborn baby? Or a newborn baby animal?

Katie Comes Home

43

44

45

Shopping with Katie

47